Contemporary Beer
Neon Signs

By Robert Swinnich

Published by

P.O. Box 69
Gas City, IN 46933

ISBN #0-89538-063-3

Table of Contents

Brewery Neons

Other Neons

Acknowledgments

My thanks to my brother James Swinnich for his photographs that made this book possible.

Pricing

As in all collectibles, buy only what you like and can afford. Try to buy the best whenever possible. Pricing is a necessary evil in any collection. Ask a hundred collectors and dealers for a price on a particular neon and you will probably get a wide range of answers. Prices vary because of geographic location, availability, age, visual appeal and other variables. Prices also vary as new signs are discovered or a warehouse of multiples are found. Signs from the past ten years are fairly plentiful and usually reasonably priced, with a few exceptions. The older the sign, the more likely it has been destroyed and the harder it is to locate outside the area, but when located should be reasonably priced because of low demand. Popularity plays a large part in prices (the more popular the sign, the higher the price.) The most popular signs seem to be the ones which incorporate pictures or logos into their signs. As you see, the manner of pricing is not an easy task and can vary substantially in different parts of the country, but hopefully with more knowledge, study and experience, the field will mature until there is uniform pricing.

Background on the Neon Sign

A good source of information about the early use of neon in the advertising field can be found in the old magazine "Signs of the Times." It was a monthly magazine published for the Sign Trade. It is an excellent look into the past of neon signs and other types of advertising signs and how they evolved. I own about 50 of these magazines from 1920's through the 1940's and always try to purchase them when they are available.

Neon came to the U.S. in the early 1920's as an advertising medium. Prior to that, as far back as the late 1800's, neon was being developed by several different scientists, one being Georges Claude. Claude sold licenses to sign businesses all across the U.S. The picture is from my private collection and it is from one of these licensers. It is porcelain over steel and measures 6" x 50" long.

It didn't take long for the Brewery Companies to see the potential in this advertising medium.

As these ads show, beer signs were being made by many local sign shops. Huge roof top signs to window signs were becoming popular. By the 1940's, neon beer signs were being made in large quantities and the window brewery neon as we know it was in full swing.

As technology advances, like the electronic transformer becoming available, the quality and intricacy of the neon sign of today will outshine the neon of yesteryear.

C

Beer Neons As A Collectible

What makes a good collectible? Should your purchase be viewed as an investment or just as a collection? First, you should consider if you like the field or times you wish to collect. Neon signs are a medium primarily used for advertising. Large outdoor neons are a fantastic form of advertising. However, to collect them is very impractical. They are not easily moved, very expensive, and too big for most of us to display. So, we must move indoors, to the smaller, less expensive window neons. Well, as you know, there are a large number of these. You can drive by many stores and see the windows full of business signs; i.e. . . . Eat at Joe's, Ed's Cleaners, Mel's Diner and so on. You will agree, an area too vast to even think of collecting. Also, it would be impossible to trade information to standardize the field. However, Brewery (BEER) Neons have all the ingredients for an item to make a very good collectible. They have a history that can be traced; a small number of manufacturers, the availability of signs (scarcity of older and limited editions of newer unusual signs,) and they have a national or regional appeal depending on the Brewery. Original sizes and original colors can be documented. Research can be done on the Brewery or the manufacturer to find out more about odd or unusual signs. Over the years a price structure can be formed, based on supply and demand. All these factors can add up to the Beer Neon finding a niche of its own in the collectible field now and in the future.

The only two ingredients that are missing is a uniform accurate grading and pricing system and you, the collector. It takes a person who loves a group of items (such as beer neons) and is willing to establish information and a network of buying, selling, trading and restoring.

This is only a brief look into beer neons. No attempt is made to include every brewery neon produced for every company. There are thousands of different beer neons with many variations. It is intended to start to explore beer neons as a collectible field and try to inform and to save the remaining early neons before they are destroyed. Most neons were originally given to bars to advertise their brands. As prices have risen, the bars are more accountable for their signs, even with the closing of the bars. Because neons were never sold to the public until very recently (the Breweries now sell neons through gift catalogs) they are somewhat difficult to obtain, especially the early ones. Breakage is another consideration when trying to obtain an older neon. Every year a few more are lost or flicker out for the last time and an unknowing storekeeper discards it forever. Defunct Breweries is another reason some neons are getting scarce. All of these factors, along with personal preference, such as color, design, national or local breweries, should be considered when building a collection along with personal preference, such as color, design, national or local breweries.

Cleaning And Caring For Your Neon

Neon signs are made of glass. Glass, which means you have to handle them carefully, VERY CAREFULLY!! If you have gotten them home safely from an auction, flea market, bar or your friends house, it might need a little attention. First, check for breaks in the tubing, worn cords or switches that have been removed. If there is a problem, do not plug it in. A break in the tubing means you must take it in for repair to a qualified neon technician. One break can cost from $25 to $65. As you can see, if there is more than one break, it can be expensive. So make sure you check the sign thoroughly before you purchase it. Power cords are often frayed or gone on older signs. They should be replaced by a qualified person, before operation, along with the switch which is often worn out. If all these things seem to be fine and your sign doesn't light, the problem might be in your transformer. A new transformer can be put on an old sign, but the cost can be high. Again, you must take your sign to a neon shop and they can test your transformer. If you want to avoid all of this, have them plug in your sign before you buy it. Also, if there is a dark spot in the tubing or the sign flickers, there is a more serious problem. It is either the transformer or the gas is showing impurities, which has to be repumped by a neon technician. Always check the transformer for a black tar substance.

If you have bought a neon that is working but is greasy and dusty it can be cleaned at home if you are very careful. Start by unplugging the sign and placing it on a level surface. The tubing can be cleaned with simple glass cleaner and paper towels. DO NOT press on the tubing! If the sign is very greasy, it might take an SOS pad to remove stubborn grease. Rub lightly! Spray with cleaner and wipe with paper towels. The transformer can be cleaned in the same manner. Allow the sign to dry thoroughly before plugging in. Overnight is the best length of time.

Trouble Shooting

Not Working
1. The switch on transformer is bad.
2. Transformer is bad.
3. Tube is broken.
4. Gas is discharged.
5. Power cord is bad.

Flickering
1. Transformer is going bad.
2. Gas has to be discharged.
3. Electrode is bad.

Dark Spots
1. Gas has impurities in it.

NOTE: Not all neon tubing can be repaired. It has to be replaced by the section. It can get expensive.

Shipping

This article appeared in the June 1940 issue of "Signs of the Times." As you can see, the method of shipping Beer Neons was as important to the neon business then as it is today. The method then was wire-bound wood crates. Today the preferred method is cardboard boxes. Most have a cardboard inner liner with the neon sign stapled to it and then small squares of foam glued to cardboard and the whole thing slips into a sturdy outer cardboard box. Smaller signs are packed back to back in the same carton. The cartons are sometimes packed on a pallet and shrinked wrapped 10-15 at a time. There is some breakage in shipping, but for the most part it is kept to a minimum.

Safe Delivery . . . Guaranteed
Signs of the Times
June 1940

This article is offered with the thought that SIGNS *of the Times* readers might obtain some help from a discussion of our experiences with the causes and prevention of breakage in sign shipments. As a producer of point-of-sale luminous-tubing displays, our company is devoted exclusively to the manufacture of quantity signs for both national and regional advertisers. We ship our signs direct to the advertisers' dealers and we are responsible for each of our signs until that sign is received by the dealer *in good order.* We guarantee safe delivery, and we pride ourselves on the manner in which all our signs are prepared for shipment.

To insure the safe delivery of small luminous-tube signs and displays, they must not only be properly designed and built, but they must also be properly packed in a manner acceptable to the carrier. As most of these signs are shipped by Railway Express, that company has made a careful investigation of the methods adopted by the manufacturers, and this investigation has done much to reduce the enormous breakages which caused all of us so much trouble in the past.

As quantity luminous-tube displays became more popular, the box manufacturers were called in and aided with their suggestions until today the percentage of breakage in the shipment of these signs is as it should be -less than 3 percent. In bringing this about, it was found that breakages resulted from at least one of the following causes:

1. Improper handling of the sign by the express company employees.
2. Inability to see at a glance that the package contains glass tubing.
3. Lack of space allowance in the crate.
4. Improper method of fastening sign inside of crate.
5. Improper support of tubing and lack of sufficient supports.
6. Defect in the manufacture of the tubing itself.
7. Breakage in the opening of the crate by the dealer receiving it.

Express-company employees have been cautioned as to the fragile nature of luminous tubing. Very little, if any, breakage can be traced to improper handling of these signs in shipment. However, trucks used by the express company are designed for maximum loading, and when the truck is nearly empty, or loaded with light packages, the springs of the trucks do not function properly with the result that the sign might receive unusual abuse over bumpy streets, and that is probably where the most damage is done.

For more than seven years, we have had success with shipping crates having the following features:

1.   Sides and top of the crate are constructed with slats of sufficient strength and width. These slats should be spaced so that the sign is easily seen by those who handle it. The mere fact that the sign is visible will insure careful handling.

2.   Sufficient free space must be allowed at sides, top and ends so there will be no danger of breakage in handling. Allow at least 3 inches.

3.   If the sign is of the cabinet or box type the cabinet should be held to the bottom of the crate with metal angles, using sufficient length and number of screws to insure against shifting or loosening of the sign through shipment. The express company prefers to have the sign cushioned with sponge rubber of excelsior pads to take up severe shocks.

If sign is of the skeleton type, transformer should be packed in a separate box. Skeleton tubing should be wired to double corrugated boards having a suitable wood frame. The crate should be constructed with grooves in ends so that corrugated board will be centered in crate, allowing proper spacing on both sides. This crate also should be of the open-slat type.

4.   For signs to be shipped, use at least one -third more supports for the tubing. This precaution is a preventive measure and no one will criticize you for it, but you will be surely "brought on the carpet" if the supports become loose or drop off in shipment.

5.   It is our belief that some signs are accidentally broken through carelessness in opening the crate. We use the wire-bound type, known as the "Rock Fastener" type of crate, as this type of crate saves its cost by the ease with which the sign can be packed.

6.   Provide sufficient warning labels on top, sides and ends. Labels are inexpensive and should be used liberally.

7.　　　The cord and chains supplied with the sign should be securely wired to the crate and not placed where they might damage the tubing.

If, after following these methods, your breakages are more than 3 percent, look to your methods of manufacture. Perhaps the tubing is weak at the point of breakage. Possibly the tubing is not centered in the housings. Careful investigation on your part should locate your trouble.

Remember, the ability to ship these signs and have them arrive unbroken will not only help you to keep your present customers, but will also help you secure new customers. To be absolutely safe, call in a good reliable box manufacturer.

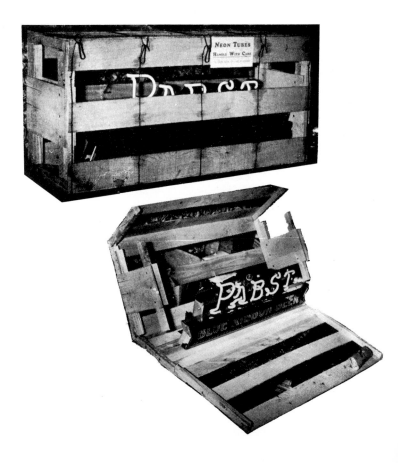

Transformers By Companies

1. Actown-Everbrite, Spring Grove Ill. Current
2. Acme Electric & Mfg. Co. Cuba NY. 1930's
3. Belts, Jersy NY 38
4. Betts & Betts NYC NY 36
5. Canatsey Elect. Mfg. KC MO 33
6. Dongan Elect. Mfg. Detroit Mich. 32
7. Eisler Engineering Newark NJ 36
8. France Mfg. Co. (Franceformers) Cleveland Ohio
9. Gardner Elect. Mfg. Emeryville Calif. 39
10. GE. Schenectady NY 32
11. Jefferson Elect. Co. Bellwood Ill. 32.
12. Light Elect. East Orange NJ. 36
13. Montroy Elect. Mfg. LA Calif. 33
14. National Trans. Co. Paterson MK 38
15. Outdoor Lighting Co. Jersey City NJ 37
16. Reco Reynolds Elect. Co. Chicago Ill. 36
17. Red Arrow Irvington NJ 36
18. Sola Elect. Co. Chicago Ill. 36
19. Thordarson Chicago Ill. 33
20. Transco West Columbia SC.
21. Westinghouse Pitts. PA 36
22. Webster Elect. Racine WIS 37

The year after the location is the first year of production. Some are still in business today. The most popular transformer used by the sign companies seem to be the Franceformers by Scott and Fetzer of Fairview Tenn. Some imports are being used more frequently. Also the new electronic transformers are starting to show up in smaller counter signs.

L

Rarity Guide

1	Rare
2	Hard to Find
3	Few Signs Around
4	Can Be Found
5	Common (Easy to find)

Explanation of Transformer Terms

Cat - Catalog number

Ser - Serial number (date)

Pri - Primary voltage

Hrz - Hertz

Sec - Secondary voltage

Ma - Milliamps

V - Volts

Va - Volt Ampere

W - Watt

Brewery - Amstel

Colors - Red, White, Gold

Notice Extras - Plastic Rings

Labels - Universal Elect. Sign
      Co. Maspeth NY

Transformers - Franceformer,
cat 7520/W 7/ser 0392/pri
120v/60hrz/185va/7500v/
20ma/France Div. Scott & Fetzer
Co. Fairview, TN

App. Frame Size - 24" x 17 1/2"

App. Date - 1992

Rarity - 5

Value - $75 - $125

Brewery - Anheuser Busch

Colors - Red, White, Blue

Labels - Item #765-125/ LA1558/Everbrite Sign Inc. South Milwaukee WI 531172 LA 1000

Transformers - Embossed ANHEUSER BUSCH INC. Brewers of Budweiser St. Louis MO Franceformer cat 9030/FM 9/ ser 07 84/pri 120/ 60hrz/ 270va/sec 9000/30ma/France Division Scott & Fetzer Fairview TN 37062

App. Frame Size - 19 1/2" x 21 1/2"

App. Date - 1984

Rarity - 4

Value - $75 - $125

A lot of neon in this sign. Double letters "LA" and a double ring make it very likely to be broken when found.

2

Brewery - Ballantine

App. Date - 1960's

Colors - White, Green, Red

Rarity - 4

Transformers - 7,500 volt not original. This sign was part of a warehouse find. There were hundreds discovered probably from a cancelled order or just not distributed. There were other designs, but all were basically the same with the 3 interloped rings. They stood for body, purity and flavor. Most of these signs were found with no transformers.

Value - $125 - $200

Brewery - Ballantine Beer

Colors - Red, White, Green

Transformers - New Trans.
runs on 9,000v

App. Frame Size - 10 1/2" x 39"

App. Date - 1962

Rarity - 2

Value - $125 - $200

Brewery - Becks

Colors - White, Red

Labels - Becks spelled out in big 4" letters and the German Spelling of Beer "Bier". Nice little sign.

Transformers - Not original but will run on a 6,000v

App. Frame Size - 19" x 10 1/2"

App. Date - 1980's

Rarity - 4

Value - $75 - $125

Brewery - Anheuser Busch
    Budweiser

Colors - Red, Ice Blue

Labels - Item # 054-535

Transformers - Cat 7530/FM 8/
ser 681/ pri 120v/60hrz/225va/
sec 7500v/30ma/France Division Scott & Fretzer Fairview, TN 37062

App. Frame Size - 14" x 19 1/2"

App. Date - 1981

Rarity - 3

Value - $125 - $200

A nice slogan neon from Budweiser. Once very plentiful but are getting harder to find. Nice script writing.

Brewery - Anheuser Busch
   Budweiser

Colors - Red, White, Ice Blue

Transformers - 9,000 v not found will original trans.

App. Frame Size - 28" x 19 1/2"

App. Date - 1990

Rarity - 2

Value - $250+

Spuds, a very popular character for a short time. He has been discontinued and the sign will continue to rise in price. A lot of neon on this sign.

Brewery - Anheuser Busch Budweiser

Colors - White, Green

Labels - Property of ANHEUSER BUSCH Budweiser Shamrock #05 4-556 6hrz neon Harbor City CA

Transformers - Type 61612W Mfg Oct 86/va 180/ pri 20/ 60hrz/sec 6,000/ma 30/ Everbrite Electric Signs.

App. Frame Size -24" x 27"

App. Date - 1986

Rarity - 3

Value - $200 - $250

Great looking shamrock. Seem to be many around, but hard to purchase one. Also same version with Bud Light inside shamrock.

Brewery - Anheuser Busch
Budweiser

Colors - Red, White, Blue,
Yellow

Transformers - Actown indoor
model F6-4044/pri 120v/60hrz/
225va/sec   9,000v/25ma/
Actown Electrocoil Inc. Spring
Grove, IL USA

App. Frame Size -19" x 21"

App. Date - 1990's

Rarity - 2

Value - $250+

Brewery - Anheuser Busch
Budweiser

Colors - Red, White, Blue,
Cream

Labels - UL Actown Indoor

Transformers - Model #3993/
prim120v/60hrz/270va/sec
9,000v/30ma/Spring Grove IL
USA

App. Frame Size - 21" x 18"

App. Date - 1992

Rarity - 2

Value - $250+

Very nice figural Bud Man. Most collectors prefer this sign because Budman is spelled out.

Brewery - Anheuser Busch
Budweiser Bottle

Colors - Red, (white
underplate)

Labels - ANHEUSER BUSCH
Item H051-281 Mt. Vernon IL
62864

Transformers - Franceformer
cat 6030/fm 6/ser 04 88/pri
120v/60hrz/180va/sec 6,000 v/
30ma/Scott & Fetzer

A very large bottle. Outlined in
red neon with a plastic label. On
the plain side, but nice never the
less.

App. Frame Size - 43" x 13"

App. Date - 1987 - 1988

Rarity - 2

Value - $250+

Brewery - Anheuser Busch
Budweiser

Colors - Red, White, Blue

Labels - Everbrite Electric Sings Inc. Greenfield, Milwaukee, Wis. 53172

Transformers - Embossed Anheuser Busch Brewers of Budweiser, Busch and Michelob Beer. Franceformer cat 9030/fm 9/ ser 283/ pri 120v/60hrz/ 270va/sec 9,000v/30ma/France Division Scott & Fetzer

App. Frame Size - 26 1/2" x 21"

App. Date - 1983

Rarity - 5

Value - $50 - $75

Also regular Bud Light "On Tap" not on sign used for many years. Often sparks from the outside ring. Nice three color design.

Brewery - Anheuser Busch
Budweiser

Colors - Ruby Red, Green

Notice Extras - Metal eagle
and writing on frame

Labels - Brass Tag-ANHEUSER
BUSCH Inc. St. Louis MO.

Transformers - Coil type within
metal box. Very early Budweiser
sign. Transformer in core and
coil type encased in metal box,
also metal eagle logo. Unusual
colors of green and ruby red.
Very hard to find.

App. Frame Size -27" x 11"

Rarity - 1

Value - $200 - $250

Brewery - Anheuser Busch Budweiser

Colors - Ruby Red, White

Notice Extras - Metal Eagle

Labels - Mt. Vernon Neon Sign Co. Mt. Vernon, IL

Transformers - Embossed Property of ANHEUSER-BUSCH St. Louis, MO./Jefferson cat 727-351/model 015/va 150/primary 115/60cyc/sec 7500v/ma 18/ Jefferson Electric Co. Belwood, IL 18352

App. Frame Size -32 1/2 " tall

App. Date - 1950's

Rarity - 1

Value - $200 - $250

1950's vintage nice ruby red neon with metal eagle attached to frame. Before the popular bowtie sign. Note: ruby red can not be repaired. Excellent sign.

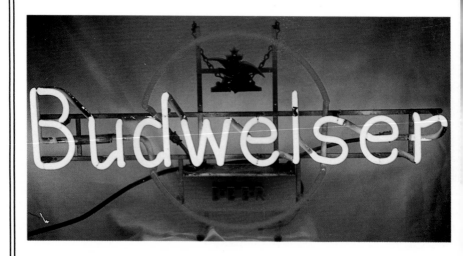

Brewery - Anheuser Busch
Budweiser

Colors - Red, White

Notice Extras - Embossed Transformer, ANHEUSER BUSCH Inc. Brewers of Budweiser, Busch and Michelob Beer St. Louis, MO.

Labels - 051-123-Bowtie Reg Universal Elect Sign Co. Maspeth, NY

Transformers - Franceformers cat 75 30 fm9/ ser 12 80 T/Pri 120/60hrz/225va/sec 7500v/ 30ma/France Division 875 Basset Road, West Lake OH 44145

App. Frame Size-15 1/2" x 29 1/2"

App. Date - 1988-1989

Rarity - 5

Value - $75 - $125

This sign used for many, many years by Budweiser. It is a commonly seen, but still very popular sign. One of the classics of neons. There is a very early version of this sign that is almost identical except it uses ruby red for bowtie with no plastic protection. The ruby red version is considered much rarer and commands a premium price.

Brewery - Anheuser Busch
Budweiser

Colors - White, Green, Pink,
Blue, Red

Labels - GHN Neon Inc. 2400
S. Vermont Ave., Harbor City
CA 90710 Telephone 310-530-
7363 Fax 310-530-1476

Transformers - Franceformer
cat 7530-7530/DB 6/Ser 0992/
pri 120v/60hrz/450 va/7500v/
30ma/Transformer embossed
ANHEUSER, BUSCH St. Louis
Mo.

App. Frame Size - 22" x 30"

App. Date - 1992

Rarity - 2

Value - $250+

One of the busiest neons, truck
palm trees, music notes. It has
everything.   Hard to find neon
and very popular.   Great graphics.   Goes with Bud commercial
on TV.

16

Brewery - Anheuser Busch
  Bud Wiser

Colors - Ruby Red, White,
  Aqua

Notice Extras - Nice up- to -date design. The bowtie is shorter and slanted for a nicer modern look. The dark aqua color is crisp and stands out over the regular green.

Labels - Everbrite, Greenfield
  WI 53220

App. Frame Size - 19" x 22"

App. Date - 1933

Rarity - 4

Value - $125 - $200

Transformers - Embossed-Anheuser Busch St. Louis MO Franceformer cat 9030/fm 601/ ser 0193/pri 120v/60hrz/ 270va/sec 9,000v/30ma France, Scott & Fetzer Co. Fairview, TN

17

Brewery - Anheuser Busch
        Budweiser

Colors - White

Notice Extras - Transformer is
        painted black

Labels - Anheuser Busch Item
#054-111 Mt. Vernon Neon Sign
Co. Mt. Vernon IL 62864

App. Frame Size - 9 1/2" x 19"

Rarity - 5

Value - $50 - $75

Transformers - Embossed
Anheuser Busch St. Louis Mo.
Franceformer Cat 4030/FM 6/
Ser 07 87/Pri 120v/60hrz/
140va/sec 4,000 v/30ma

Brewery - Anheuser Busch
Budweiser

Colors - Red, White

Transformers - Embossed Anheuser Busch St. Louis Mo. Everbrite #BL-359 Model #3849-11/pri 120v/60hrz/180va/sec6000v/30ma/Actown Electrocoil Inc. Spring Grove, IL USA1986/60 30fm/ser 08 86/2nd Franceformer sec 6,000 30mc/France S&E

App. Frame Size - 20" x 17"

Rarity - 4

Value - $75 - $125

Labels - Everbrite, Inc. Greenfield, WI 53220 #051-265LA1540

Notice Extras - The classic Bud Bowtie made into a smaller sign.

Brewery - Anheuser-Busch (Budweiser)

Colors - Ruby Red and White

Notice Extras - Metal Eagle

Labels - Anheuser Busch Inc. St. Louis Mo.

App. Frame Size - 27" x 11"

Rarity - 4

Value - $200 - $250

Transformers - Core and coil type enclosed in a metal case in back of the sign. Transformer 7500v sec.

Brewery - Anheuser Busch
Budweiser

Colors - Red, White

Labels - Item #540-305 LA-2419/Everbrite Greenfield WA 53220 Rate Mfg. April 2,1990 Insp. 2081

Transformers - Everbrite premium indoor gas tub transformer/Everbrite part #BL359-2 Model NO. 3991-11/pri 120v/ 60hrz/180va/sec 6,000/volts 30ma/secondary mid point grounded. Actown Electrocoil Inc. Spring Grove IL Made in USA.

App. Frame Size -10" x 28"

App. Date - 1990

Rarity - 5

Value - $75 - $125

A vertical sign mounted on black plexiglass. A unique sign and easily found.

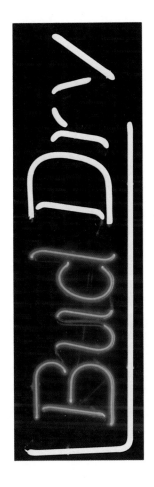

Brewery - Anheuser Busch Budweiser

Colors - White, Green, Cream, Ruby Red

Labels - Budweiser Country LA 051-926/GHN Neon Inc. 31 Columbia Ave. Aliso Viejo, CA

Transformers - Embossed ANHEUSER BUSCH St. Louis MO 3 position dimmer switch France former cat 9030/fm 601/ ser 0693/pri 120v/ 60hrz/ 270va/sec 9,000v/30ma/Scott Fetzer Co.

App. Frame Size - 26" x 16"

App. Date - 1993

Rarity - 4

Value - $125 - $200

Great new design and use of old type colors. Description: The red is a deep ruby red and the green has the 50's look. The country lasso intertwines with the familiar Bowtie design. The built-in dimmer switch is a great touch. A well thought design.

Brewery - Anheuser-Busch
(Budweiser)

Colors - Ruby Red

Labels - Mt. Vernon Sign Co. of
Illinois.

Transformers - cat 727-351/
model 015/va.150/primary v.
115/60cyl/secondary 7500v/
ma 18/The transformer is embossed "Property of Anheuser
Busch St. Louis, Mo"

App. Frame Size - 32 1/2"

App. Date - 1950

Rarity - 4

Value - $200 - $250

Brewery - Anheuser Busch
Budweiser

Colors - Red, Blue, Orange,
White

Notice Extras - Has extended bracket on top for easier hanging on wall. Descripton: One of many of sports neons the companies are producing. This is an action sign as the basketball is going through the net as shown by the blue neon off to one side.

Labels - Embossed Anheuser Busch, St. Louis MO

App. Frame Size - 23" x 19"

App. Date - 1992

Rarity - 4

Value - $75 - $125

Transformers - Franceformer cat 7530/fm 6/ser 0192/pr 120v/60hrz/225va/sec 7,500v/ 30ma/Division of Scott & Fetzer Co. Fairview TN 37062

Brewery - Anheuser Busch
Budweiser

Colors - Red, White, Blue

Notice Extras - Embossed
Transformer Anheuser BUSCH
St. Louis, MO.

Labels - Everbrite Electric Signs
Inc. S. Milwaukee Wisc. 53173

Transformers - Franceformer
cat 6030/fm 6/ser 0786/pri
120v/60hrz/180va/sec 6,000v/
30 ma

App. Frame Size - 16" x 32 1/2"

App. Date - 1986

Rarity - 5

Value - $50 - $75

Used by Anheuser Busch for
many years. Comes in slight
variations.

Brewery - Anheuser Busch
Budweiser

Colors - Red, White, Blue

Labels - Everbrite Electric Signs
Inc. S. Milwaukee Wisc. 53172
LA 1000

Transformers - Embossed
ANHEUSER BUSCH St. Louis
MO/Franceformer cat 6030/FM
6/ser 07 86/pri 120v/60hrz/
180va/sec 6,000v/ 30ma/
France Division Scott & Fetzer
Fairview, TN 37062

App. Frame Size - 12" x 20"

App. Date - 1986

Rarity - 4

Value - $75 - $125

Smaller version of your classic
Busch Mt. three colors and line
underneath make for a cute little
sign.

Brewery - Anheuser Busch Budweiser

Colors - Red, White, Blue

Labels - 1. Everbrite Inc. Green Field Wis. 53220 LA 1000 2. Item No. 206-7555 LA 2223

Transformers - Everbrite part #BL 355 Model #385-11/ pri 120v/ 60hrz/225va/sec 7,500v/ 30ma/Actown-Electrocoil Inc. Spring Grove, IL Made in USA Embossed ANHEUSER BUSCH St. Louis MO.

App. Frame Size - 18" x 31 1/2"

App. Date - 1990

Rarity - 4

Value - $75 - $125

This is the newer version of Busch Mt. three colors but top Mt. unprotected. This sign also has been downsized.

27

Brewery - Carling

Colors - White

Labels - Mt. Vernon Neon Sign Co. Mt. Vernon, IL

Transformers - Franceformer cat 7530/fm 7/ser 269/pri 120v/60cy/240va/sec 7,500v/ 30 ma/France Manufacturing Division/The Scott & Fetzer Co. Westlake Made in USA OH/Embossed Carling

App. Frame Size - 31" x 6 1/2"

App. Date - 1969

Rarity - 3

Value - $75 - $125

Plain sign, but hard to find in one piece because of length. Only one color.

Brewery - Carling

Colors - Red, White

Notice Extras - Embossed Transformer, HANGING ONLY

Labels - The countryman incorporated 36th Southern Covington KY Property of Carlings Brewing Co. Cleveland OH, St. Louis MO. Belleville, IL.

Transformers - ARJAC Products Inc. Rochester NY 60 cycles/pri 115v/amps 150/sec v 7500/ sec ma 18

App. Frame Size -12" x 20"

Rarity - 4

Value - $75 - $125

Two signs, the early version with ruby red tubing and later version with just red neon.

Brewery - Carling Black Label Brewing Comp. of America Cleveland OH

Colors - White

Labels - Operate on 115v ac only The Countryman Incorporated Co. 36th and Southern Corington KY

Transformers - no markings

App. Frame Size -19" x 13"

App. Date - 1951

Rarity - 2

Value - $125 - $200

An early Carling sign with a plastic face. Nicely made but could have used more color. Nice sign.

Brewery - Anheuser Busch
      Carlsberg

Colors - Green

Labels - Everbrite, Inc.
Greenfield, WI 53220 LA 1000
Item No. 506-725

Transformers - Embossed
ANHEUSER BUSCH St. Louis
MO/Everbrite model no. 3849-
11/Pri 120v/ 60hrz/180va/sec
6,000v/30ma/Actown
Electrocoil, Inc. Spring Grove, IL
Made in USA

App. Frame Size -24" x 11 1/2"

App. Date - 1988-1989

Rarity - 4

Value - $75 - $125

Nice all green sign with shamrock as an accent.

Brewery - Colt 45

Colors - Yellow, Ice Blue

Labels - Everbrite 296 Greenfield, MO 53220 Item No. 0542

Transformers - Everbrite #bl-295/model #3849-20/pri 120v/ 60hrz/225va/sec 9000v/25ma/ Actown Electrocoil Spring Grove, IL

App. Date - 1980

Rarity - 4

Value - $75 - $125

Colt 45 Horseshoe sign, very good looking neon. Used for many years. Colt 45 also has a sign without horseshoe.

Brewery - Coors

Colors - Red, White, Gold

Labels - Everbrite Inc. Greenfield, WI 53220 Union Label

Transformers - Franceformer, cat 9030 FM/ser 1188/pri 120v/ 60hrz/270va/sec 9,000v/ 30ma/France Scott & Fetzer Co./Fairview TN 37062

App. Frame Size - 25" x 19"

App. Date - 1989

Rarity - 4

Value - $75 - $125

Color combination makes this a good looking sign. Gold liner is expensive to repair on this sign.

Brewery - Coors

Colors - Red, White, Gold

Labels - Everbrite Greenfield, WI 53320 Briteway Signs a division of Everbrite Inc. P.O. Box 576, Lacrosse WI 54602 608-781-8700

Transformers - Valmot Electric cat no. 9030NI/120v/60hrz/270va/sec 9,000v/30ma

App. Frame Size -25 1/2" x 19"

App. Date - 1989

Rarity - 4

Value - $75 - $125

Almost same as other Extra Gold sign but "Draft" is different.

Brewery - Coors

Colors - Red, White, Gold

Labels - 1988 Adolph Coors Co. Golden Co. 80401 Brewer of fine Quality Beers since 1873

Transformers - Franceformer TN 37062/cat 90/30fm/1287/pri 120v/60hrz/270va/9,000/ 30ma

App. Frame Size -22" x 23"

App. Date - Jan. 1988

Rarity - 4

Value - $75 - $125

Large bold sign with stand-out colors.

Brewery - Coors

Colors - Ice Blue

Labels - Everbrite Inc. Union Label

Transformers - (Newer) 7530FM/ser 0988/120v/60hrz/ 225va/sec7500v/30ma (Older) Property of Aldoph Coors Co. #L910158000 Silver Bullet Everbrite Hon Kong type T7512W/Mfg. Sept. 86/sec 7500/30ma/GHN Neon Co. Harbor City

App. Frame Size -14" x 27 1/2"/ 17" x 26 White background

App. Date - 1988-89/1986

Rarity - 4

Value - $125 - $200

Used for many years for Coors. A very popular sign as the graphics on the plastic part of sign make the can appear it is flying. Two versions with the plastic insert can being only difference. The newer version has a sleeker silver can insert. The older has a white plastic back plainer insert.

Brewery - Coors

Colors - Red, White

Labels - Coors item #91-0155200 E4663 Mt. Vernon Neon Mt. Vernon IL 62864

Transformers - Franceformer cat/9030fw/ser1089/pri 120v/60hrz/870va/sec 9,000v/30ma

App. Frame Size -27 1/2" x 19"

App. Date - 1989

Rarity - 5

Value - $50 - $75

Common Sign, Straightforward.

Brewery - Coors

Colors - Red, Ice Blue

Labels - Property of 1988 ADOLPH Coors Co., Golden Co. 80401 Brewer of fine quality beers since 1873 Item No. L910158500 Coors Beer Reg. GHN Neon Co. Inc. Harbor City, CA 213-538-7363

Transformers - Hong Kong Everbrite Electric signs Inc. GHN Neon Co. Inc. Harbor City, CA/ type T7512W/mfg Dec. 87/va 225/pri 120/hrz 60/sec 7500/ ma 30

App. Frame Size -15" x 29"

App. Date - 1982 - 1988

Rarity - 5

Value - $50 - $75

Common Coors Mountain. Used for many years. Comes in different sizes.

Brewery - Fort Schuyler

Colors - Red, White

Transformers - No Transformer,
7,500v

Nice early sign, with a nice scroll
of neon on the bottom sign.

App. Frame Size - 13" x 24"
Thin wire frame

App. Date - 1950's

Rarity - 2

Value - $200 - $250

Brewery - Fosters

Colors - Red, Blue, Gold

Notice Extras - On blue
              Plexiglass

Labels - Universal Elect. Sign Co.
Maspeth NY

Transformers - Franceformer
cat 7530W7/ser 0291/pri 120/
60hrz/225va/sec 7500/30ma/
France Division of Scott & Fetzer
Fairview TN 37062

App. Frame Size -22 1/2" x 26"

Rarity - 4

Value - $125 - $200

A lot of neon on a blue plexiglass
back. Makes for a very good looking sign. Also seen without "On
Tap" on sign.

Brewery - Genesee

Colors - Pink, White, Green

Transformers - Franceformer, cat 7520HM3/ser 170/pri 120v/ 60cy/165va/sec 7500v/20ma

App. Frame Size -25" x 15"

App. Date - 1970

Rarity - 4

Value - $125 - $200

Similar to Genesee On Tap with nice colors. Used for many years by Genesee.

Brewery - Genesee

App. Frame Size -13" x 23"

Colors - Green, Yellow, Pink

Rarity - 4

Transformers - 7,500

Value - $125 - $200

An older version of a common sign. The 50's type colors are great on this sign. Very appealing.

Brewery - Genesee

Colors - Red, White

Labels - Sign #2 Universal Sign Maspeth NY

Transformers - Franceformer cat 7520WM/ser 1286/pri 120v/60hrz/165va/sec 7500v/20ma/France Scott & Fetzer

App. Frame Size - 24" x 13"

App. Date - 1986

Rarity - 5

Value - $75 - $125

A slight variation of the more common sign. The "Beer" is in the same line of neon as the outside ring and is often broken when found.

Brewery - Genesee

Colors - Red, White

Labels - Universal Eelect. Sign Co. Maspeth NY #19814 GB Co. Roch NY

Transformers - Franceformer, cat 7520/W 7/ser 0189/pri 120v/60hrz/165va/sec 7500v/20ma

App. Frame Size - 13 1/2" x 25"

App. Date - 1989

Rarity - 4

Value - $75 - $125

"Beer" is in line of neon circle and very often found broken.

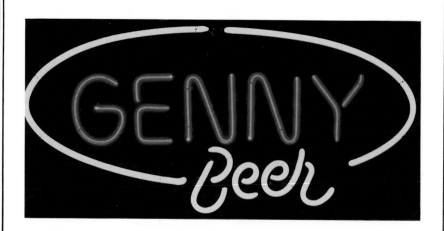

Brewery - Genesee

Colors - Red, Ice Blue

Labels - Universal Elect. Sign Co. Maspeth, NY

Transformers - Jefferson Electric a division of Magnetek Inc. cat 75-351-710/pri 120v/60hrz/ 150va/sec 7,500/20 ma/A8704

App. Frame Size -24" x 13"

App. Date - 1988

Rarity - 4

Value - $75 - $125

Almost the same as "Genny Beer" except Light is on its own circuit. A nice look to this sign.

Brewery - Genesee

Colors - Red, White, Blue

Labels - Universal Eelect. Sign
      Co. Maspeth NY

Transformers - Franceformer,
cat 7530W 7/ser 0391/pri 120v/
60hrz/225va/sec 7500v/30ma/
France Div. Scott & Fetzer Co.
Fairview, TN 37062

App. Frame Size - 14" x 30"

App. Date - 1991

Rarity - 3

Value - $200 - $250

Probably the nicest Genesee sign
figural. Mug and four colors
make for a good sign. Hard to
find.

Brewery - Genesee

Colors - White, Gold, Green

Transformers - Franceformer, cat 7520 H/ser 371/120v/ 60hrz/165/va/7500v/20ma/ Scott & Fetzer

Good colors and getting harder to find with Cream Ale version.

App. Frame Size -25" x 15"

App. Date - 1971

Rarity - 4

Value - $75 - $125

Brewery - Genesee

Colors - White, Green

Transformers - Original? ARJAC Prod. Inc. Roch NY Luminous Jube Transformer Made in USA/cat 7518-HF/cyc 60/pri 115v/amps 150/sec 7500 v/sec MA18

App. Frame Size -12" x 25"

App. Date - 1950's

Rarity - 1

Value - $200 - $250

Early Genesee sign. You don't see many signs with the words "On Draft" in Neon.

Brewery - Genesee

Colors - Red, White

Labels - Universal Eelect. Sign Co. Maspeth NY

Transformers - Franceformer, cat 7520 WM/ser 0386/pri 120v/60hrz/165va/7500v/ 20ma/France Div. Scott & Fetzer Co. Fairview, TN

App. Frame Size -22" x 13"

App. Date - 1986

Rarity - 4

Value - $75 - $125

Plain, straightforward sign.

Brewery - Gibbons

Colors - Red, Blue

Transformers - Not original 7,500v

Rarity - 4

Value - $125 - $200

Good Design with "G" incorporated in sign. Nice color and sign is difficult to find.

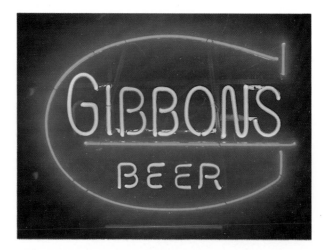

Brewery - Hamm's

Colors - White

Labels - Universal Eelect. Sign
Co. Maspeth NY

Transformers - Franceformer,
cat 7520W/ser 0784/pri 120v/
60hrz/165va/sec 7500v/20ma
Division of the Scott & Fetzer
Fairview TN 37062

App. Frame Size- 8½" x 24½"

App. Date - 1984

Rarity - 2

Value - $50 - $75

Straightforward, Hamms is a
fairly popular sign, 3½ " script
letters.

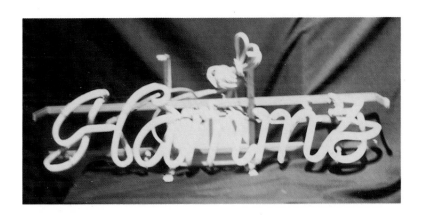

Brewery - Hamms Not Original New

Colors - Red, White

Transformers - 9,000v not original

App. Frame Size - 25 1/2" x 21"

App. Date - 1992

Rarity - 3

Value - $250+

This is a newly made up sign, but is a nice figural. The sign is well made.

Brewery - Heineken

Colors - Green White

Notice Extras - Newer version has plastic around outside ring.

Labels - Universal Elec. Sign Co. Maspeth, NY

Transformers - Franceformer cat 7520WM/ser 1186/pri 120v/ 60hrz/165va/sec 7,500/20ma/ France Division Scott & Fetzer Fairview TN 37062//both signs have same transformer cat 7520W7

App. Frame Size-14½" x 28½"
14" x 28¾"

App. Date - 1986/1991

Rarity - 3

Value - $125 - $200

Popular sign with collectors. The design did not change but a plastic piece was added to protect the outside ring on the newer version.

Brewery - Iron City

App. Frame Size -18 1/2" x 18"

Colors - Red

Rarity - 4

Transformers - Original? cat 7520F/ser 1272/pri 120v/ 60hrz/165va/sec 7500v/20ma France and Fetzer Co. Westlake Made in USA Ohio

Value - $75 - $125

This sign has two rings, one in the middle and one outer ring missing. It loses about half the value in this condition.

Brewery - Iroquois

Colors - Red, White

Transformers - 7,500 not original separate

A nice early Buffalo, NY Iroquois sign. Like the slogan "The Bold Beer."

App. Frame Size - 20" x 14"

App. Date - 1950's

Rarity - 2

Value - $200 - $250

Brewery - Iroquois

Colors - Red, White

Transformers - 7,500 probably Hanging

App. Frame Size - 24" x 16"

Rarity - 2

Value - $125 - $200

"Have an Iri" Logo makes this a nice sign and very popular. Also seen without "On Tap."

Brewery - Keystone (Coors)

Colors - White, Gold

Labels - 1992 Coors Brewing Co. Golden Colorado 80401 Item #L 910554101

Transformers - 120v/60hrz/ max 2/amp max 140w/Everbrite Inc. Greenfield WI 53220

App. Frame Size - 17" x 26"
Plastic Back

App. Date - 1992

Rarity - 4

Value - $75 - $125

Another product of Coors Keystone. Sign is mounted on clear plexiglass and "Beer" is plastic. Also has a larger version where "OPEN" is added in neon at bottom.

Brewery - Killians (Coors)

Colors - Red, Green

Labels - Property of 1988 Adolph Coors Co. Golden Co. 80401 Brewery of fine quality beer since 1873. Item No L 910160051 Killians Red Everbrite electric Signs-GHN Neon Co. Inc. Harbor Cit CA 213-530-7363

Transformers - Franceformer cat 7530W/ser 1287/pri 120v/ 60 hrz/225va/sec 7500v/30ma/ France Divison of Scott & Fetzer Co. Fairview TN 37062

App. Frame Size-14 1/2" x 22 1/2"

App. Date - 1988

Rarity - 4

Value - $75 - $125

Nice color combination, also can be found with shamrock neon accent above "S" on Killians (like shamrock on Carlsburg)

Brewery - King Cobra
Anheuser Busch

Colors - Red, White

Labels - Item #755-155 Everbrite Electric Signs S. Milwaukee WI 53172

Transformers - Embossed ANHEUSER BUSCH cat 75306/ ser 12-86/pri/120v/60v/225va/ sec 7,500v/30ma/Franceformer

App. Frame Size - 15 1/2" x 25 1/2"

App. Date - 1986

Rarity - 5

Value - $50 - $75

Brewery - Kochs

Colors - Red

Transformers - ACME Electric cat no. L-207/ser P59/pri 115v cy 60/sec 7500v/sec ma 18/va 150/Luminous tube and transformer/Cuba NY A-21550 Made in USA

App. Frame Size - 38$1/2$" x 6"

App. Date - 1959

Rarity - 2

Value - $200 - $250

This long sign mounted on glass rods is very hard to find unbroken. Over 3ft. long. Displays nice if you have the room.

Brewery - Koch's

Colors - Red, White, Blue

Notice Extras - "O and C" on Koch's darker because of gas leak or impurities.

Labels - Property of Fred Koch Brewery, Punkiry, NY

Transformers - France Manuf. Co. Westlake, OH 120v/60cyl/ 165va/sec 7500v/20ma

App. Frame Size-15$1/2$" x 25$1/2$"

Rarity - 2

Value - $200 - $250

This is known as the diamond sign from Kochs. It's also seen without "Beer" in sign and also with "On Tap" replacing "Beer." Shows very nice because of the three colors.

Brewery - Koch's

Colors - White, Yellow

Transformers - Franceformer, cat 7520 F/ser 561/pri 120v/ 60cycl/165va/sec 7,500/20ma/ France Man. Co. Cleveland OH USA

App. Frame Size - 10" x 26 1/2"

App. Date - 1961

Rarity - 2

Value - $200 - $250

Unusual Kochs sign from Dunkirk NY. Hard to find without any breaks. One of the nicest Kochs signs.

Brewery - Kochs

Colors - Red, White, Gold

Transformers - Franceformer, cat 7520 F/ser 174/pri120v 60cyl/165va/sec7,500v/20ma/ Scott & Fetzer Co.

App. Frame Size - 24" x 12"

Rarity - 2

Value - $125 - $200

Three colors on this sign makes it a nice looking sign for a relatively single design.

Brewery - Koch's Brewery
           Black Horse

Colors - Red, Green

Transformers - No Transformer
6,500v

App. Frame Size - 15" x 23 1/2"

App. Date - 1950's

Rarity - 2

Value - $200 - $250

A very hard sign to find. It is a Koch's Brewery Brand from Dunkirk, NY. Straightforward sign.

Brewery - Labatts

Colors - Red, White, Blue

Labels - Everbrite Greenfield WI 53220 Date MFG Nove 19, 1991 UL/Union

Transformers - Actown model #F6-3992/pri 120v/60hrz/ 225va/sec 7500/30ma/Actown Electrocoil Inc. Spring Grove IL USA

App. Frame Size - 31" x 14"

App. Date - 1991

Rarity - 3

Value - $75 - $125

Brewery - Labatts

Colors - Red, White, Ice Blue

Labels - Worden Traditional Neon Display Co. Inc. 1412 Deleglise St. P.O. Box 179 Antigo WI 54409

Transformers - Actown Model #FG-3851/pri 120v/60hrz/ 270va/sec 9,000/30ma/Actown Electrocoil Inc. Spring Grove IL Made in USA

App. Frame Size-30½" x 16½"

App. Date - 1988-1989

Rarity - 3

Value - $75 - $125

A straighter line version of the Labatts Maple leaf. Still popular and can be found.

Brewery - Labatts Blue

Colors - Red, White, Blue

Labels - Worden Glass 0 331 96 Traditional Neon 1412 Deleglise St. Antigo WI 54409

Transformers - Actown #FG-3992/pri 120v/60hrz/225va/sec7500v/30ma/Actown Electrocoil Spring Grove IL

App. Frame Size - 24" x 27"

App. Date - 1990's

Rarity - 4

Value - $125 - $200

The newer larger version of Labatt's Maple Leaf. Very popular but can be found.

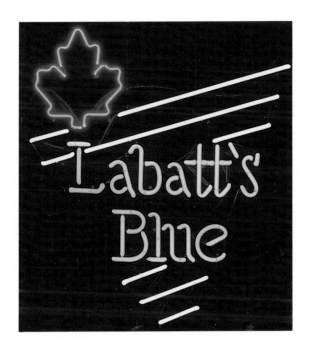

Brewery - Leisy's (Cleveland OH)

Colors - Red, Lime Green

Notice Extras - Hanging on double wire frame.

Labels - Painted on transformer property of Leisy's Brewing Co.

Transformers - Embossed cat 727-351/cap 150va/pri 115v/60 cycles/secondary 7500v/18ma/ Midpoint of Sec. Grounded Jefferson Electric Co. Bellwood IL USA 218739

App. Frame Size -29 1/2" x12 1/2"

App. Date - 1951

Rarity - 2

Value - $200 - $250

Straightforward sign, simplistic is best sometimes.

Brewery - Little Kings (Ohio)

Colors - White, Green

Labels - Universal Elect. Sign
Co. Maspeth NY

Transformers - Franceformer,
cat 7520/W 7/ser 0392/pri
120v/60hrz/185va/7500v/
20ma/France Div. Scott & Fetzer
Co. Fairview, TN

App. Frame Size - 18 1/2" x 29"

App. Date - 1980's

Rarity - 4

Value - $75 - $125

A great looking sign and it is
a little hard to find.

Brewery - Matts

Colors - Red, White

Transformers - Franceformer cat 7520WM/ser 281T/120v/ 60hrz/165va/sec 7,500/20ma/ France Division Scott & Fetzer Westlake OH 44145

App. Frame Size - 30" x 14½"

App. Date - 1981 - 1976
(2 signs)

Rarity - 5

Value - $50 - $75

Nice looking Banner type sign. Common.

Brewery - Michelob

Colors - Red, White, Yellow

Labels - Everbrite Inc.
Greenfield, WI 53220

Transformers - Embossed
ANHEUSER BUSCH St.Louis
MO/Everbrite #BL-355/Model
#3850-11/pri 120v/60hrz/
225va/sec 7,500v/30ma/
Actown Electrocoil Inc. Spring
Grove IL USA

App. Frame Size - 18" x 20"

App. Date - 1989

Rarity - 5

Value - $75 - $125

Brewery - Michelob

Colors - Red, White

Notice Extras - Embossed Transformer Everbrite Elect.

Labels - Item 663171 Michelob Light Mt.Vernon Neon Sign Co. Mt. Vernon IL 62864/Everbrite Elect. Signs Inc. South Milwaukee WI 53172 Item No. 663-175 same transformer

Michelob Ribbon sign, common. Has been changed in recent years to new sign.

App. Frame Size - 23" x 24"

App. Date - 1979 - 1981

Rarity - 5

Value - $50 - $75

Transformers - Embossed ANHEUSER BUSCH Brewers of Budweiser, Busch, and Michelob Beer/Franceformer cat 7530 FM 9/ser 579/pri 120v/60hrz/225 va/sec 7,500/30ma/France Scott & Fetzer Co. 875 Bassett Rd.West Lake OH 44145

Brewery - Lowenbrau Miller

Colors - Ice Blue, Yellow

Labels - (Small) 21-52479 Miller Brewing Co. Milwaukee, WI USA 1982 Universal Sign Co. Maspeth, NY (Large) 21-52674 Miller Brewing Co. Milwaukee WI USA 1984

Transformers - (Large) Franceformer cat 7530WI/ser 03 84/120v/60hrz/225va/7500v/30ma/Scott & Fetzer TN

App. Frame Size - 28" x 20"/ 18" x 17"

App. Date - (L) 1984//(S)1982

Rarity - 4

Value - $75 - $125

This sign comes in two sizes. Both identical except size. Plastic Lion.

LÖWENBRÄU

Brewery - Miller

Colors - Yellow

Labels - 17-14267 Miller Brewing Co., Milwaukee WI

Transformers - Inside plastic (transistor type)

App. Frame Size - 31 1/2" x 11"

App. Date - June 4, 1990

Rarity - 4

Value - $125 - $200

Bottle is plastic with neon outline very sharp looking.

Brewery - Miller

Colors - Light Purple, Yellow, Green

Labels - Code #04-53061 Miller Brewing Co. Milwaukee WI USA '87' Everbrite Elect. SIgns Inc. S. Milwaukee WI 53172

Transformers - Everbrite part #BL-264/Model 3851-20/pri 120v/60hrz/270va/sec 9,000v/ 30ma/Actown Electrocoil Inc. Spring Grove IL Made in USA

App. Frame Size - 23" x 20½"

App. Date - 1987

Rarity - 2

Value - $250+

Made by Miller Brewing Co. Matilda Bay Cooler is a very nice figural sign. The sign has been discontinued and it is believed the company took back the signs and destroyed them. This sign should become a very desirable sign. The purple also has a tendency to fade out, so good examples are hard to find.

Brewery - Miller

Colors - Red, White

Notice Extras - Blinker

Labels - (S) Lakeside Plastics
C1497-1798/(L) Miller Brewing
Co. Milwaukee WI USA 1982
Itme #01-52671 Mt. Vernon
Sign Mt. Vernon IL 62864

Transformers - (Same Transformer for both small and large
size.) Franceformer cat 5030
303022/ser 573/pri 120v/
60cyl/260va/sec 500v/30ma/
Flashed sec 3000v/30ma

App. Frame Size - 19 1/2" x 26"
16" x 21 1/2"

App. Date - (S) 1978/(L) 1986

Rarity - 4

Value - $75 - $125

This blinking sign comes in two
sizes. Some collectors like the
blinking actions. Again this type
of sign does have a spark or snap
noise because of the ring.

Brewery - Miller

Colors - Red, White

Notice Extras - Newer has plastic outer ring. Old is metal

Labels - Third sign Universal Elec. Sign Maspeth Ny 01-52477 Miller Brewing Co., Milwaukee WI USA 1978

Common sign used for many years. There is a blinking version. Most of these signs spark or snap because of outer ring.

App. Frame Size - 16" x 21 1/2"

App. Date - 3rd 1978-1980

Rarity - 5

Value - $50 - $75

Transformers - (1st Sign) Franceformer cat 7520PM/ser 867/pri 120v/60cyc/165va/sec 7500v/20ma (2nd Sign) Jefferson cat 727-351/model 501/pri 120v/sec 7500/60cyc/20ma (3rd Sign) Franceformer cat 7530 WIA/ser 280/pri 120v/60hrz/225va/7500v/30ma/Scott & Fetzer

Brewery - Miller

Colors - Red, White, Yellow

Notice Extras - Box marked 1-MHL Bowling Ball No. 01-532-53247

Labels - #01-53247 Miller Brewing Company Milwaukee, WI USA 1991 Universal Elec. Sign Co. Maspeth, NY

Transformers - Franceformer, cat 9030 FM 2/Sr 0891/pri 120v/ 60hrz/270va/sec9,000/ 30ma/France Division of Scott & Fetzer Co. Fairview TN 37032

App. Frame Size - 28" x 20 1/2"

App. Date - 1991

Rarity - 2

Value - $200 - $250

Great sign for bowlers. Action type with pins flying everywhere. Would have made a nice flashing sign.

Brewery - Miller

Colors - White, Yellow

Notice Extras - Neon line in base behind plastic encased in plastic for bar.

Labels - Miller Brewing Co. Milwaukee WI USA Item #01-14344E Mt. Vernon Neon Mt. Vernon IL 62864

Transformers - Encased (transistor type)

App. Frame Size - 9 1/2" x 18"

App. Date - 1991

Rarity - 3

Value - $75 - $125

This is a counter neon all encased on 3 sides in plastic. The figural bottle just plugs in and can be lifted out for quick change. A very neat little sign.

Brewery - Miller

Colors - Red, Gold

Labels - Universal Elect. Sign Co. Maspeth NY 01-53333 Miller Brewing Co, Milwaukee WI USA 1989

Transformers - Jefferson cat #750 151 701/pri 120v/60hrz/ 225va/sec 7,500v/30ma/A 8706

App. Frame Size - 26" x 15 1/2"

App. Date - 1989-1991

Rarity - 5

Value - $50 - $75

Common sign. The Gold in Miller is a special expensive glass tubing and is not easily repaired if broken.

Brewery - Miller

Colors - Red, White, Green

Labels - Mt. Vernon Sign Co. Mt. Vernon IL 62864

Transformers - Franceformer cat 7530 M7/ser 1089/120 pri/ ser 1089/60hrz/225va/sec 7,500v/30ma

App. Frame Size - 24" x 12"

App. Date - 1989

Rarity - 4

Value - $75 - $125

This is the Miller High Life with a Shamrock accent. Very good 3 color sign.

Brewery - Miller

Colors - (1st) Yellow, Red, White
(2nd) Red, Yellow

Labels - (1st) Miller Brewing Co.
Milwakee WI USA item 17-53018
Mt. Vernon Neon Sign Co. Mt.
Vernon IL 62864 (2nd) Same except Item #17-53240E

Transformers (1st) Franceformer cat 9030 FM 7 Ser 0689 pri
120v/60hrz/270va/sec 9,000/
30ma (2nd) 7530W7 0890/120v/
60hrz/225va/7500v/30ma/
(Both) Scott & Fetzer France Fairview TN 37062

App. Frame Size -
(1st) 491/2" x121/2"
(2nd) 42" x 91/2"

App. Date - (1st) 1987-89
(2nd)1990

Rarity - 4

Value - $125 - $200

Two sizes: The larger version has all neon 3 colors. The shorter version "Genuine Draft" is in plastic 2 colors. The larger version has a more detailed guitar.

Brewery - Miller

Colors - Red (White plastic lights)

Labels - #01-52-937 Miller Brewing Co. Milwaukee WI USA 1985 Universal Elec. Sign Co. Maspeth NY

App. Frame Size - 26 1/4" x 17"

App. Date - 1985

Rarity - 4

Value - $75 - $125

Popular Miller sign with slogan in plastic and Miller in large double letters.

Brewery - Miller

Colors - Red, White

Labels - Universal Elect. Sign Co.

Transformers - 90 30FM3/ser 11 82/pri 120/60v/270va/sec 9,000/30ma/France Scott Fetzer TN

App. Frame Size-10 1/2" x 27 1/2"

App. Date - 1982

Rarity - 4

Value - $75 - $125

This sign comes in two versions. This one says "Welcome to Miller Time." The other says "Welcome it's Miller Time." A slogan used by Miller for a few years in the 1980's.

Brewery - Miller Highlife

Colors - White, Red

Labels - Miller Brewing Co. Milwaukee WI USA Item #01-53380/Mt. Vernon Neon Mt. Vernon IL 62864

Transformers - France cat 9030FM7/ser 0593/pri 120v/60hrz/270va/sec 9,000/30ma/Scott & Fetzer Co.

App. Frame Size - 27" x 18"

App. Date - 1993

Rarity - 3

Value - $125 - $200

A very nice baseball neon sign from Miller. Ball almost appears to be in flight. A must for baseball fans.

Brewery - Lite Miller

Colors - Ice Blue, White

Labels - Universal Elect. Sign Co. Maspeth NY 57-52-938

Transformers - Franceformer, cat 7520/W 7/ser 0392/pri 120v/60hrz/185va/7500v/ 20ma/France Div. Scott & Fetzer Co. Fairview, TN

App. Frame Size-12 1/2" x 16 1/2"

App. Date - 1986

Rarity - 4

Value - $50 - $75

Brewery - Miller Lite

Colors - White, Ice Blue

Notice Extras - Small size

Labels - Universal Elec. Sign Co. Maspeth NY

Transformers - Franceformer, cat 5030 WI/ser 0288/pri 120v/ 60hrz/160va/sec 5,000v/30ma

App. Frame Size-12 1/2" x 16 1/2"

App. Date - 1988

Rarity - 5

Value - $50 - $75

Brewery - Miller Lite

Colors - Red, White, Blue

Labels - Mt. Vernon Neon Sign Co. Mt. Vernon IL 57-5230 Miller Brewing Co. Milwaukee WI USA 1977/Universal Electric Sign Co. Maspeth NY 1987

App. Frame Size - 21" x 17"

App. Date - 1977 - 1987

Rarity - 5

Value - $50 - $75

Transformer - Franceformer cat 7530 FM 1/ar 120 v/60hrz/sec 7,500v/ser 1277/225va/30ma/ 0187/France Fairview TN 37062/875 Basset Rd. Westlake OH 44145/Scott & Fetzer/Same Transformer 11-88

Brewery - Miller Lite

Colors - Blue, White, Gold

Notice Extras - Box #57-53261

Labels - Universal Elec. Sign Maspeth NY

Transformers - cat 75 30 FM 701/pri 120v/60hrz/225va/ser 7,500v/30ma

App. Frame Size-24$\frac{1}{2}$" x 26$\frac{1}{2}$"

App. Date - 1992

Rarity - 4

Value - $125 - $200

Football helmet figural with plexiglass backing. Rectangle outlined in neon. Came with stickers such as "Monday Nite Football" and NFL football teams. A great sign for football fans.

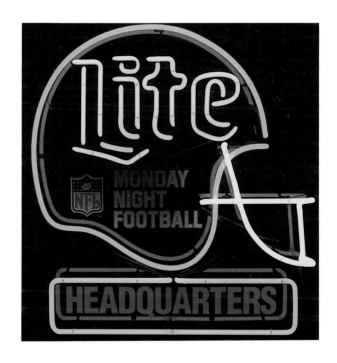

Brewery - Miller Lite

Colors - Purple, Green, Blue, Orange

Notice Extras - 57-53372 Box " x57-53553

Labels - Universal Elec. Sign Co. Maspeth NY

Transformers - Franceformer, cat 9030 FM 701/ser 0792/pri 120v/60hrz/270va/sec 9,000/ 30ma/France Scott & Fetzer Fairview TN 37062

App. Frame Size - 23 1/2" x 21"

App. Date - 1992

Rarity - 2

Value - $250+

Beautiful Palm Tree on this sign. Very popular sign and is relatively hard to find. I have heard the original purple ring is being replaced by pink because of purple fading, so hang on to the purple rings.

Brewery - Miller Lite

Colors - Red, White, Blue, Green

Labels - Miller Brewing Co. Milwaukee WI USA Item #57-53186E Mt. Vernon Neon Mt. Vernon IL 62864

Transformers - cat 90 30 FM 7/ser 0490/120pri/60v/30ma/220 va/sec 9,000v/France Division Scott & Fetzer

App. Frame Size - 24" x 22"

App. Date - 1990

Rarity - 4

Value - $125 - $200

Double letter Lite and 4 colors make a good looking sign. Also comes in a Burgess sign.

Brewery - Miller Meister Brau

Colors - Red, Yellow

Labels - 29-52940 Miller brewing Co. Milwakee WI USA 1986 Universal Electric Sign Co. Maspeth, NY

Transformers - Type T7512W/ MFG-Jan 86/va 225/pri 120 hrz/60/sec 7,500/30ma/Universal Electric Sign Co. Inc. Made in Hong Kong

App. Frame Size - 23" x 18

App. Date - 1986

Rarity - 5

Value - $50 - $75

Common sign straightforward.

Brewery - Miller Reserve

Colors - White, Gold

Labels - Miller Brewing Co. Mt. Vernon Neon Item #32-53671 Mt. Vernon IL 62864

Transformers - Franceformer cat 7530 W7/ser 0992/pri 120v/ 60hrz/225va/sec 7,500v/30ma

App. Frame Size - 22 1/2" x 16"

App. Date - 1992

Rarity - 4

Value - $75 - $125

Figural Eagle perches above Miller. The sign comes on a plexiglass backing and also on a metal frame.

Brewery - Molson

Colors - Ice Blue, Gold

Labels - Universal Elect. Sign
Co. Maspeth NY

Transformers - cat 7530 W 7/
ser 0590/pri 120v/60hrz/
225va/sec 7,500/30ma/Scott &
Fetzer

App. Frame Size - 10" x 27"

App. Date - 1990

Rarity - 4

Value - $125 - $200

Also comes in "On Tap" instead
of "Beer & Ale."

Brewery - Moslon Canadian Loon

Colors - Red, White, Gold, Blue

Labels - Universal Elect. Sign Co. Property of Martlet Imorting Co. Reston VA

Transformers - Franceformer, cat 90 30 FM 7/ser 2 92/pri 120v/50ma/270va/sec 9,000v/30ma

App. Frame Size - 24" x 25 1/2"

App. Date - 1992

Rarity - 2

Value - $250+

Very popular with Canadian collectors is the Molson Loon sign. Have seen this sign with and without (on tap.)

Brewery - Moosehead

Colors - Red, White, Green, Yellow

Notice Extras - This sign is a newer sign, Older original is larger in size.

Labels - Autokeg Systems 111 Belton Drive Spartanburg IL 29304

Transformers - Uses 2 transformer. Franceformer cat 7530 FM 7/ser 0286/120v/60hrz/ 225va/sec 7500v/30ma

App. Frame Size - 21" x 27"

App. Date - 1986

Rarity - 2

Value - $250+

Moosehead is a favorite among collectors. Excellent figural sign. Has been made in 3 sizes. This is the medium size. The smaller version is a very cute sign. Very popular.

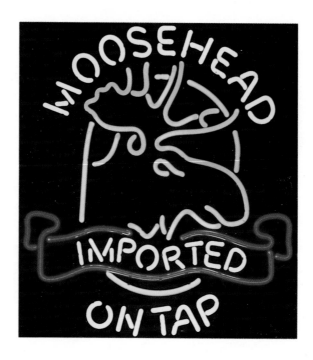

Brewery - Nando

Colors - Red, White, Yellow

Notice Extras - Plastic insert

Labels - Universal Elect. Sign
Co. Maspeth NY

Transformers - cat 9030 FM 7/
ser 08/90/pri 120v/60hrz/
270va/sec 9,000v/30ma/France
Division of Scott & Fetzer
Fariview TN 37062

App. Frame Size - 19" x 39"

App. Date - 1990

Rarity - 4

Value - $125 - $200

Nice figural bottle, plexiglass outlined in neon. Large sign.

Brewery - Natural Light

Colors - White, Ice Blue

Labels - Universal Elect. Sign Co. Maspeth NY Item #463-173

Transformers - Franceformer cat 6030 FM5/ser 8 80T/pri 120v/60hrz/180va/6,000sec/ 30ma/France Scott & Fetzer OH

App. Frame Size - 21 1/2" x 22"

App. Date - 1980

Rarity - 5

Value - $50 - $75

Common sign "Light" in plastic. The newer, smaller version is almost the same but the part of outer ring was left off.

Brewery - Old Milwaukee

Colors - White

Notice Extras - Plastic face and neon run around it. Hanging only.

Labels - 1965 Jos. Schlitz Brewing Co. Milwakee, Brooklyn, KC, Tampa

Transformers - Sticker on back of transformer Old Milwaukee Americas Light Beer/mod # 9T6144125671-62cy/pri 120/va 200/sec 6,000/ma property of Ios. Schlitz Brewing Co. Milwaukee, WI USA

App. Frame Size - 19" x 15"

App. Date - 1965

Rarity - 2

Value - $75 - $125

1960's sign not a spectacular sign, but very neat in appearance. Could have been made nicer with a few colors added.

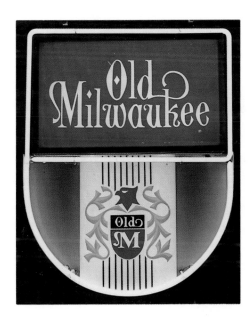

Brewery - Old Topper

Colors - Blue, Gold

Transformers - 7,500v not original

Nice older sign. Prone to damage with 2 outside rings not protected. Probably a local sign hard to find.

App. Frame Size-17-1/2" x 17-1/2"
No frame

App. Date - 1950's

Rarity - 2

Value - $200 - $250

Brewery - Old Vienna

Colors - Red, White, Blue

Labels - Universal Elect. Sign Co. Maspeth NY

Transformers - Franceformer, cat 7530 W1/ser 0488/pri 120v/ 60hrz/225va/sec 7,500v/30ma/ Divison Scott & Fetzer Co. Fairview TN 37062

App. Frame Size - 21" x 18"

App. Date - 1988

Rarity - 4

Value - $125 - $200

Just say OV slogan with figural maple leaf. Three colors make this a good looking sign.

Brewery - Old Vienna

Colors - Red, Ice Blue

Labels - Universal Elect. Sign Co. Maspeth NY #058091 Century Importers Inc. Baltimore MD 1989

Transformers - Franceformer, cat 7520W7/ser 0489/pri 120v/ 60hrz 165va/sec 7,500v/30ma/ Division Scott & Fetzer Fairview TN 37062

App. Frame Size - 17" x 20"

App. Date - 1989

Rarity - 4

Value - $125 - $200

Double letter OV inside figural maple leaf great looking. Sign is very popular.

Brewery - Ox Cart Standard Brewing Co.

App. Frame Size - 2ft x 14" no Frame

Colors - Pink, White, Green

App. Date - 1950's

Transformers - No transformer 7,500v

Rarity - 1

Value - $200 - $250

Older sign with no frame makes it hard to find in one piece. Great 50's colors, unusual dry beer sign.

Brewery - Olympia

Colors - Red, Ice Blue

Labels - Universal Elect. Sign
      Co. Maspeth NY

Transformers - cat 727-151-
704/pri 120v/60hrz/225va/sec
7,500v/30ma/Jefferson Electric
Litton Bellwood, IL 60104

App. Frame Size - 20" x 24"

App. Date - Newer

Rarity - 5

Value - $50 - $75

Nice Double letters on OLY and
plastic ring around neon.

Brewery - Pabst

Colors - Red, Blue

Labels - Universal Elect. Sign Co. Maspeth NY Pabst No. 01013 Property of Pabst P2323

Transformers - Franceformer, cat 7520/W 7/ser 0392/pri 120v/60hrz/185va/7500v/ 20ma/France Div. Scott & Fetzer Co. Fairview, TN

App. Frame Size - 19" x 21"

App. Date - 1981

Rarity - 5

Value - $75 - $125

A sign seen a lot that has been around for years. Does have good colors and shows well.

Brewery - Pabst

Colors - Red, White, Blue

Labels - Everbrite Electric Signs Inc. S. Milwaukee 53172

Transformers - Everbrite (Hong Kong) type T912H/mfg April 83/ va 270/pri 120/60hrz/30ma/ sec 9,000/South Milwaukee

App. Frame Size - 22 1/2" x 23"

App. Date - 1983

Rarity - 3

Value - $125 - $200

This sign is the same as Pabst Ribbon sign with the slogan, "This is the Place," added. A common sign made a little nicer.

Brewery - Pabst

Colors - White, Blue

Labels - Metal Tag Pabst US Pat #3,056,221 use with 7,500 volt 30ma transformer. p-436 sign #77424 property of Pabst Brewing co. Milwaukee Nervark LA, Perria Heights

Transformers - Franceformer, cat 7530Fm10/ser 172/30ma/ pri 120v/60hrz/240va/sec 7,500/Scott & Fetzer

App. Frame Size - 11" x 35"

App. Date - 1972

Rarity - 3

Value - $125 - $200

The scroll neon around sign is a great touch and makes the sign. The sign is a change from the commonly seen Pabst Ribbon sign.

Brewery - Pabst

Colors - Red, White, Blue

Labels - Property of Pabst
P1900 Pabst #8401

Transformers - Type T751200/
60hrz/va225v/pri 20v/30ma/
sec 7,500v/

App. Frame Size - 19" x 21 1/2"

Rarity - 4

Value - $75 - $125

Pabst Blue Ribbon sign used for
many years and still popular.

Brewery - Rolling Rock

Colors - Blue, White, Green

Labels - Everbrite Date Mfg. July 3, 1991

Transformers - Actown model #FG-3993/pri 120v/60hrz/ 270va/sec 9,000v/30ma

App. Frame Size-20½" x 20½"

App. Date - 1991

Rarity - 3

Value - $200 - $250

Great Figural Horsehead, good colors. Also comes in a shamrock instead of 2 circles. Popular sign.

Brewery - Schaefer

Colors - Red, Blue

Transformers - Embossed property of Schaefer Brewing Co. Brooklyn, NY/Franceformer cat 752-H ser 961/pri 120v/60cy/ 150va/sec 7,500v/20ma/France man. Co. Cleveland OH USA

App. Frame Size - 10" x 16" Electrodes extend over frame

App. Date - 1961

Rarity - 4

Value - $50 - $75

Small sign but has charm. Electrodes do extend over frame, so be careful when handling sign.

Brewery - Schlitz

Colors - Red

Labels - Metal tag on sign form
5-1 1968 Jos. Schlitz Brewing
Co. Milwaukee and other cilips
The beer that made Milwaukee
famous.

Transformers - Property of Jos.
Schlitz Brewing Co. Milwaukee
WI USA cat 5030FM6/ser 375/
pri 120v/60hrz/160va/sec
5,000v/30ma/France Division
The Scott G. Fetzer Co. 875
Bassett Rd. Westlake OH 44145
Made in USA

App. Frame Size - 23" x 9"

App. Date - 1968

Rarity - 5

Value - $50 - $75

Common sign with nice script
writing.

Brewery - Schlitz

Colors - White

Labels - The beer that made Milwaukee famous. Union Label

Transformers - Property of Jos, Schlitz Brewing Co. Milwaukee WI USA cat 6030F/ser 670/pri 120v/60cyc/190va/sec 6,000/ 30ma/France Manufacturing Scott & Fetzer Co. Made in USA OH

App. Frame Size -10 1/2" x 33 1/2

App. Date - 1970

Rarity - 4

Value - $50 - $75

Double lettering of Schlitz helps this otherwise plain sign.

Brewery - Schlitz

Colors - Gold, White

Labels - (Smaller Size) Metal Tag, Form 590 use with 7,500 18ma transformer property of Jos. Schlitz Brewing Co. Milwaukee WI Breeveries at Milwaukee, WI and Brooklin NY The beer that made Milwaukee famous. Sticker, Everbrite Electric Signs. Only difference in large sign, form 550

Transformers - (sep)

App. Frame Size -21" x 23"/ 21" x 16"

App. Date - Older

Rarity - 5

Value - $50 - $75

Brewery - Schlitz Stroh's Brewery

Colors - Blue, White

Labels - Everbrite Inc. 2/96 Greenfield, WI 53220 Stroh Brewery Co. 80724 Neon Sign

Transformers - Everbrite part no. BL295/model #3849-20/pri 120v/60hrz/180va/sec/6,000v/ 30ma/Actown Electrocoil Inc. Springrove IL

App. Frame Size - 23" x 18"

App. Date - 1989

Rarity - 2

Value - $125 - $200

Nice figural head of bull. There is also a nicer full body bull which is very difficult to obtain.

Brewery - Schmidts

Colors - Red, White

Transformers - Scott & Fetzer 875 basset cat 7520WM/ser 1-81T/pri 120v/60hrz/165va/ 7,500v/20ma

App. Frame Size - 23" x 11"

App. Date - 1981

Rarity - 4

Value - $75 - $125

Double ring Schmidt's hard to find when 1 ring is not broken.

Brewery - Sharps Miller

Colors - Red, Yellow, (White underplate)

Notice Extras - Flashing Action Plastic label neon behind

Labels - Miller Brewing Company Item #10-53575 Mt. Vernon Neon

Transformers - Franceformer, cat 430 1530 1530 E6R23/ser 03 93/pri 120v/60hrz/245va/ 4000v constant/30ma constant/ 1500v flashed/30ma flashed/ Scott & Fetzer Co. Fairview, TN 37012

App. Frame Size - 30 1/2" x 9"

App. Date - 1993

Rarity - 3

Value - $125 - $200

A non alcoholic beer from Miller. A great figural flashing sign. Three way flasher makes it appear bottle opens.

Brewery - Simon Pure

Colors - Red, Green

Transformers - Not original separate 7,500v

App. Frame Size - Non frame
25" x 12"

Rarity - 4

Value - $75 - $125

Earlier sign with nice colors from Buffalo NY Brewery usually found without transformer.

Brewery - Stag

Colors - Red, White, Yellow

Labels - Mt. Vernon Neon Sign
Co. Mt. Vernon IL

Transformers - Franceformer,
cat 7530FM2/ser 867/pri 120v/
60cyl/240va/sec 7500v/30ma/
The France Man Co. Westlake
USA OH

App. Frame Size - 21 1/2" x 18"

App. Date - 1967

Rarity - 3

Value - $75 - $125

Colors are great on this sign.
Hunters like this sign.

Brewery - Stegmaiers

Colors - Red

Labels - Round white label on sign, Stegmaier W5-89

Transformers - Not original 7,500v

App. Frame Size - 24" x 9"

Rarity - 3

Value - $75 - $125

App. Frame Size-24 1/2" x 21 1/2"

Brewery - Strohs

App. Date - 1986

Colors - White, Red

Rarity - 3

Notice Extras - Plastic backing on mug

Value - $125 - $200

Labels - Everbrite Electric Sign Inc. South Milwaukee WI 53172 #80154 Neon Sign Strohs Brewing Co. 86

This sign is backed by a mug shaped piece of plexiglass. Very good neon, with the exception of an electrode that sticks way out in back of sign and is easily broken off in transporting.

Transformers - Franceformer cat 9030FM3/ser 1182/pri 120v/60hrz/270va/sec 9000v/30ma/France Division Scott & Fetzer Fairview TN 37062

Brewery - Strohs

Colors - Red, White

Labels - Universal Elect. Sign
Co. Maspeth NY

Transformers - Webster Racine
WI type 3L7520PS/code F81A/
pri 120/60hrz/sec 7,500/pri a
1.8/sec a .020

App. Frame Size - 23" x 11"

Rarity - 4

Value - $50 - $75

Your basic Strohs sign with an
"Open" sign attached.

Brewery - Strohs

Colors - Red

Transformers - Franceformer, cat 7520WM1/ser 12 78/60hrz pri 120v/165va/sec 7,500/ 20ma/Scott & Fetzer Co. 875 Baseet Rd. Westlake OH 44175

App. Frame Size - 11" x 23"

App. Date - 1980

Rarity - 5

Value - $50 - $75

Brewery - Tuborg

Colors - Red

Labels - Universal Elect. Sign
Co. Maspeth NY

Transformers - Type E912W/
60hrz/180va/pri 120v/sec
9000v/20ma/Universal Electric
Sign Co. Inc. Made in Hong Kong.

App. Frame Size - 18" x 16"

Rarity -4

Value - $75 - $125

Even though only one color it has
a nice visual appeal with Scroll
of neon incorporated in it.

Brewery - Utica Club

App. Frame Size-19½" x 24½"

Colors - Red, White, Blue

Rarity - 4

Transformers - France Manuf. Co. West Lake OH Division Scott & Fetzer Co. cat 9020HM/pri 120/60cyl/190va/sec 9000v/ 20ma/mounted front

Value - $75 - $125

Good colors. An exciting sign but fairly common.

Brewery - Utica Club

Colors - Red, White, Blue

Notice Extras - Hanging Transformer

Transformers - Embossed WEST END BRG Franceformer cat 9020 H4/ser 972/pri 120v/ 60cy/790va/sec 9000v/20ma/ France Scott & Fetzer Co. West lake OH

App. Frame Size - 16" x 23"

Rarity - 4

Value - $75 - $125

Another nice sign with three colors from Utica Club. Circle is often found broken.

Brewery - Watneys

Colors - White

Transformers - Webster type 3L6020P11/code186D/60hrz pri 120v/sec 6000v/pri 1.3a/sec1020a

App. Frame Size - 21¹/₂" x 15"

App. Date - 1986

Rarity - 3

Value - $125 - $200

This sign is mounted on a barrel shaped piece of plexiglass which really makes it a nice sign. An unsual sign and one worth saving.

Brewery - Wurzburger

Colors - Red, Ice Blue

Transformers -Hanging separate Transformer. Uses 7,500v

Nice two color sign with two end caps of neon. Also seen without "on tap."

App. Frame Size-10 1/2" x 27 1/2"

App. Date - 1992

Rarity - 2

Value - B

Brewery - Wurzburger

Colors - Red, White

Transformers - Not original. Runs on 7,500 volts

App. Frame Size - 27" x 10½"

App. Date - 1970's

Rarity - 4

Value - $75 - $125

Design - Smirnoff

Colors - Red, Plastic Smirnoff in White

Labels - Property of Heublein Inc. Farmington CT, Call for Smirnoff Item #061943

Transformers - Type T512W/ Mfg June 88/pri 1120/60hrz/ sec 5,000/30ma/Everbrite Electric Signs, GHN Neon Co. Harbor City GA

App. Frame Size - 32" x 17"

App. Date - 1950's

Rarity - 2

Value - $125 - $200

Smirnoff is in plastic. A small sign that could be used on counter.

Design - Home of the 99 cent Draft

Colors - Red, White, Blue, Yellow

Transformers - 9,000v not original.

App. Frame Size - 31" x 32"

App. Date - 1980's

Rarity - 4

Value - $125 - $200

This sign was made for a chain of restaurant/bars with 1950's decor. Nice large sign in shape of a beer mug. Nice for home bar with no brand name represented.

Design - Ice Cream Cone

Transformers - 7,500v

A classic design used since the 1940's for ice cream parlors. The name of the store is usually incorporated into the signs.

App. Frame Size - 32" x 17"

App. Date - 1950's

Rarity - 2

Value - $125 - $200

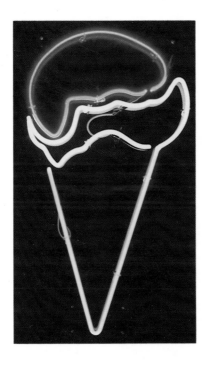

Neon Clocks, Clocks, Clocks

As soon as neon was used for advertising, it was incorporated into clock designs. From building tops, to store fronts, to windows and counter tops, thousands of neon clocks were produced from the 1930's through present day. There were shapes in octagons, squares, rectangles and circles, double ring and single ring clocks. Advertising and non-advertising clocks were used in stores all across the nation. The early clocks were mostly metal cases and a glass front using the core and coil type transformers. As plastic became popular it was used for the front of the clocks. It was easily formed and could be easily changed for different advertising faces. A couple of the different types of clocks would be; the Aztec design, where a thin piece of metal, die cut design, is placed over a double ring clock to block out some of the outer ring of neon to give a nice effect. The spinner type is another kind of neon clock. It has a plastic round disc attached to the clock motor and spins as the clock moves. It is clear plastic to the outer edge where it goes over the neon circle. It has alternating blacked out spaces. As it spins over the neon circle it appears to be spinning. This effect is also achieved by a special second hand that spins around a clock with a silk screened face that has permanently blacked out spaces on the outer glass.

As you can tell, there are many types of neon clocks. There are beer advertising neon clocks that are difficult to find. As far as prices are concerned, the range is as varied as the type of clocks. The plain non-advertising clocks start out at the low end with unpopular brand names and products and increase as the popularity of the product increases such as coca-cola, pepsi, etc. Most all neon clocks in working order start at $100 and go up. Double rings usually start at $200 and go up. The Aztec design is a more popular clock and usually starts at $500 and goes up. The spinners are usually smaller sizes and start at $200. The advertising neon clocks usually follow advertising trends. Gas and oil advertising clocks are hot. Coke and pepsi usually command a premium price. The earlier clocks are $500 and up. This is only a brief look into neon clocks which could be a book of their own. Most collectors should have at least one in their collection.

Design - Camel Cigarettes

Colors - Purple, Gold

Notice Extras - Smoking Joe Face is in plastic with neon triangle around it.

Labels - GHN Neon Inc. 2400 S. Vermont Ave. Harbor City CA

Transformers - Actown model FG - 4047/pri 120v/60hrz/150va/sec 5,000v/30ma

App. Frame Size - 23¹/₂" x 23"

App. Date - 1990's

Rarity - 2

Value - $250+

This is a very popular character sign. Although the sign is seen quite often it does not come on the market as frequently as other cigarette signs. It is popular and commands a good price.

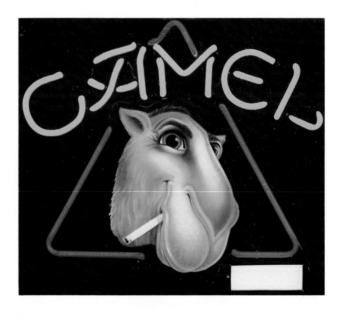

Design - Camel Cigarettes

Colors - Yellow, White

Labels - Everbrite Electric Signs S. Milwaukee 53172

Transformers - Everbrite Electric Signs Hong Kong S. Milwaukee type 17512W/Mfg. Dec 82/ 225va/pri 120/60hrz/sec 7500/ 30ma

App. Date - 1992

Rarity - 3

Value - $125 - $200

Design - Marlboro Cigarettes

Colors - Red, White

Transformers - Everbrite type E912W/Mfg. Feb. 85/180va/pri 120/60hrz/sec 9,000/20ma

App. Frame Size - 20" x 11"

App. Date - 1985

Rarity - 4

Value - $75 - $125

Figural cigarette sign. Smoke makes it appear cigarette is lit. Used for many years.

Design - Salem Cigarettes

Colors - Pink, Green, Yellow

Labels - Everbrite date mfg. May 24,1994 Union Lable 76 757901

Transformers - Actown model #FG-3992 pri 120v/60hrz/ 30ma/225va/Actown Electrocoil Inc. Spring Grove IL USA

App. Frame Size-22 1/2" x 21 1/2"

App. Date - 1991

Rarity - 4

Value - $75 - $125

Great art design sign. Some call this the sailboat sign.

Design - Coca-Cola Coke w/Ice

Colors - Red, White, Blue

Transformers - Actown model F6 - 3991/pri 120v/60hrz/ 180va/sec 6,000v/30ma/ Actown Electrocoil Inc. Spring Grove IL USA

App. Frame Size - 21" x 15"

Rarity - 2

Value - $200 - $250

Great coke neon sign. Excellent soda cup with ice. Vertical "Coke" on cup makes a beautiful sign.

Design - Pepsi Cola

Colors - Red, White, Blue

Transformers - Transco 229
Parson West Columbia SC 29169
1-800-845-1800

App. Frame Size - 26" x 18"

App. Date - 1987

Rarity - 2

Value - $200 - $250

Commonly known as the Pepsi
Bookend sign. Pepsi is very
popular and this sign is no exception. A well built sign with a
good frame around it.

Design - Pepsi Cup

Colors - Red, White, Blue

Transformers - Transco Hong Kong cat 7912W/date apr 88/ 60hrz/270va/pri 120/a 2.48/ sec 9,000v/30ma/229 Parson West Columbia SC 29169 1-1800-845-1800 or 803-796-1000

App. Frame Size - 32" x 17"

App. Date - 1950's

Rarity - 2

Value - $125 - $200

Like the other soda cup neons it is a great looking sign. Hard to find and usually is bought quickly.

Design - 7-Up

Colors - Red, White

Notice Extras - Plastic top and bottom.

Labels - Everbrite Electric Sign Inc.

Transformers - Franceformer, cat 9030FM ser 173 pri 120v/ 60cyl/270va/sec 9,000v/30ma/ France Man. Scott & Fetzer Co. West Lake Made in USA OH

App. Frame Size - 24"x 35"

App. Date - 1973

Rarity - 1

Value - $250+

This is a very 60's looking sign with top and bottom in plastic. Very bold 7-Up in middle. Nice hard to find sign.

Design - 7-Up Cup

Colors - Red, White, Green

Transformers - Actown model F6-3851 pri 120v/60hrz/270va/ sec 9,000v

App. Frame Size-27 1/2" x 14 1/2"

App. Date - 1990

Rarity - 2

Value - $200 - $250

Great looking soda cup with straw. Very nice graphics and good colors make for a nice sign. Largest of the soda cups.

Design - Corvair

Colors - White, Gold

Transformers - Separate runs on 6,000v

App. Frame Size - 231/2" x 23"

App. Date - 1990's

Rarity - 2

Value - $250+

Design - GM

Colors - Pink, White

Transformers - 9,000 v, separate transformer hangs above sign, not original.

App. Frame Size - 24" x 40"

App. Date - 1940's - 1950's

Rarity - 1

Value - $200 - $250

This dealer sign was introducing the new Hydra-Matic Drive to the GM line.

GM is in a nice hot 50's pink. It is of interest to collectors owning a Hydramatic car.

Design - Pontiac

Colors - Pink, Ice Blue

Transformers - Runs on 9,000v, not original but separate from sign.

App. Frame Size - 32" x 50"

App. Date - 1940's - 1950's

Rarity - 1

Value - $250+

This very large Pontiac dealer sign, like all car dealer signs, is very popular with collectors. The top part of this sign (the Indian head) is being reproduced. I have seen these signs sell for $1,000 at car shows. This one sold at auction for $350 in 1991.

Design - Harley Davidson

Colors - Red, White

Transformers - Transformer's not original but it does run on 2 separate transformers, both being 6,000v.

App. Frame Size-27½" x 23½"

App. Date - 1990

Rarity - 2

Value - $250+

This sign is the logo sign and is quite popular due to the interest in vintage Harley Motorcycles.

There is another Harley sign that has an eagle incorporated into the design and it is more desirable than this sign.

Design - GE Appliances

Colors - Red, Blue

Transformers - 7,500v, not original, separate hanging type

App. Frame Size - 32" x 17"

App. Date - 1950's

Rarity - 2

Value - $125 - $200

This sign incorporates the GE logo into it with appliances down below. It probably used to hang in the old mom and pop appliance store, but with the new super stores, it all but disappeared. Now can be found in small used appliance stores.

Design - Parrot

Transformers - 7,500v

This figural sign is a decorator type sign. It is used in homes or restaurants as an accent piece. The colors are great and the black plexiglass gives the sign a modern sleek look.

App. Frame Size - 34" x 14"

App. Date - 1990's

Rarity - 5

Value - $250+

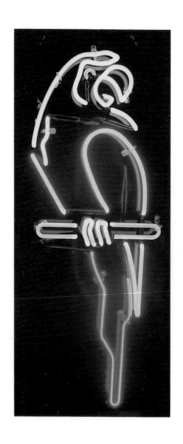

Design - Hotel Restaurant Equipment Supplies

Colors - Pink, Green

Transformers - 1,500v transformer not original.

App. Frame Size - 16" x 41"

App. Date - 1950's

Rarity - 5

Value - $200 - $250

1950's store neon sign. This sign has 4" letters. The collectable value of the sign is not great, but has greater value as a used sign for someone who is in that type of business. With a new transformer it could last another 30 years. The cost of a new sign would be close to $500.

Design - Freys Fine Sausage

Colors - Red, Blue

Labels - Label on neon tube Central Neon Sign Co. 556 Broadway, Buffalo NY Sales-Service Neon Lighting.

Transformers - Separate hanging transformer 9,000v not original.

App. Frame Size - 17" x 20" All Glass Frame

App. Date - 1960's

Rarity - 4

Value - $75 - $125

This older sign is still in use in many corner stores and deli stores. Nice design. The outer circle of neon is used as a frame with a hanging transformer.

Design - Wurlitzer Jukebox

Colors - Red, Pink

Transformers - Runs on 6,000v

App. Date - 1985

App. Frame Size- 60" x 32"

Rarity - 5

Value - $200 - $250

This is a decorator sign. It is a cardboard jukebox mounted on a plywood backing and neon accent lines. It is very appealing in daylight or at night with the neon light. I have seen a smaller version mounted on plexiglass and all done in neon. Very popular with restaurants with 50's motif.